Praise for "Th

This is poetry of the wild, ⎜ humans; Lock's poems trav estuary, woods, fields, alwa ˎˎ.ˎ˞ the complex, changing relati ˍˍˎˎ˞een human and more-than-human, and how the impact of humankind is imprinted on the earth, for better or worse. Troubling themes such as climate change are touched on lightly: in 'Melting Iceberg' she sees something *too enormous to contemplate .... as white space slides from frame to frame.* In many of these poems, life is lived on the edge, survival is not guaranteed, and the poet doesn't shy away from bringing to our attention the many ways human beings threaten and abuse the natural world, as in 'The Cruelty' and, more obliquely, in 'The final item on the news' where a saw-whet owl is displaced from a felled Christmas tree in New York and, at the same time, the poem describes a little owl found in a chimney at home. In the final part of the book, Lock expands her poetic lens, and explores mythological landscapes embedded in our collective memory.

The ancient lineage of the land surfaces in these poems, both in terms of its geology and the ways in which humans have exploited the landscape in the past, such as Devon and Cornwall's mining history. Bright vignettes of wildlife surface too: fox, swans, owls, roe deer, wasps, magpies, tracing their tracks through poems. Plants, too, bring their distinctive presences into poems; in the title poem, a child of nine wants her world only to be *her and cliff and sky,* and this deep empathy with the natural world defines Lock's poetry; fragility and resilience are held in fine balance, beauty is tough, and nothing exemplifies this more than thrift, which clings to cliff-edges and brunts the gales and salt of the sea. Displacement, entrapment, extinction: none of these themes are far away but the poet writes about them with great emotional containment, never lapsing into diatribe or sentimentality. People are displaced and abused too, as in 'At the Foundling Museum' where the poet imagines the thoughts of a mother having to give up her child.

Thrift is full of stylistic diversity; Lock sculpts her language to mirror her subject. There are stanza poems, prose poems, sequence poems and poems of patterns and shapes. Experimentation with white space seems to be a defining feature, as in 'Haar', where words float down the white space of the page, held in suspension, just like the sea-mist being evoked. This is someone who loves words that wind round her tongue and her pen: poems that beg to be read aloud. **Sue Profitt**

In Thrift, Alison Lock celebrates the vibrant life of fragile environments. These poems trace paths through moorlands and coastlands, beautifully observing details of 'stonecrop, sea-spurrey, vetch.' As you read this collection, you will shelter among ancient gritstone shoulders, meet a wolf-woman and a Highland nature goddess, and pause to share a cup of mugwort tea with women working in Cornish mines. Despite the uncertainty brought by climate change, there is always 'a brittle optimism in pale first-growths.' **Yvonne Reddick**

Here is a poem about a girl exuberant on a swing, a poem mourning the early death of a city fox, poems about walks late in the day into wildscape. Again and again, I find myself perfectly present in the pure, sharp air of places described and brought into beautiful life on the page. This is serious poetry, about all that matters in our today and more than anything about our loss of the natural world. Yes, this is serious poetry, and it is poetry that is seriously fine. **Kenneth Steven**

Thrift

Palewell Press

Thrift

Poems by Alison Lock

Thrift

First edition 2024 from Palewell Press,
www.palewellpress.co.uk

Printed and bound in the UK

ISBN 978-1-911587-80-4

A CIP catalogue record for this title is available from the
British Library.

Acknowledgements

With thanks to the many dedicated editors of the following poetry magazines and reviews, for publishing versions of these poems in this collection:

Anthropocene, Arc Magazine, Atrium, Black Bough Poetry, Blyth Spirit, Caduceus, Contemporary Haibun, Daily Haiku, Dawntreader, Empty House Press, Ethelzine, Feral Literary Magazine, Indigo Dreams Press anthology For the Silent, Ink Sweat & Tears, Macro, Maytree Press anthology, Mycelium, Nymphs, One Hand Clapping, Pennine Platform, Places of Poetry, Poetry Birmingham, Poetry Pea, *Reliquiae,* Sky Island Journal, Skylight 47, Tears in the Fence, The Beach Hut, The Galway Review, The Wild Word, Tiny Seeds Literary Journal, Words for the Wild, Writers' Cafe Magazine. "Motion, Emotion" was commended in the Welshpool Poetry Open Competition.

Dedication

For Ian

Contents

'Nature is the direct expression of the divine imagination.'
From the "Anam Cara" by John O'Donohue.

Rue

'With rue my heart is laden'. A.E. Housman.

Dawn

Now

is the calm

before the tally time

when clocks enumerate their

hourly psalms, barometers preponderate

the depth of cloud, while overnighting coals

have yet to meet the white of day. Small comforts

gained from dying flames, a floorboard's off-beat creak,

a water pipe's percussive play – is all – until you hear the

click-click jaws of the yawning dog whose yogic stretch

alerts the cat, now woken from the slumbers of a sleepy

mist to rasp her tongue in rhythmic licks that rock

and stir the runners of the rocking chair,

announcing news of morning's

shift from smoky grey

bringing a new

day into the

light.

The Monarch of Mabon   i

The fields reflect the cumulous pattern
      of cloud on the blade-cut
            silvered soil – our second harvest.

All is still. On the road
      rolls neither car nor tractor,
            but there is movement

in the hedgerow, a butterfly lands
      – The Monarch has arrived
            after her long flight.

Black-veined wings
      delineate her shape as
            she grazes on the milkweed.

A long-tongued bumble bee
      gathers nectar from the
            sun-loving foxglove.

We hold our breath, knowing
      that when evening comes
            we are drawn towards the moon

– as are the moths
      released from the hands of Mabon
            before the campion's final bow.

Melting Iceberg

It's no good looking
at a shooting star
with a fly trapped in your eye. You hear
the yawn above the skin tide
mewling and popping like a calved whale
while you spell out the words:
mastodon, sabre-toothed tiger, giant bear.
But this is mammoth, humungous, too
enormous to contemplate – at times
quiet, sometimes mute. You stare
through the classroom window, watch
dust as white space slides
from frame to frame.

Winscar

The drowned farmhouse keeps watch beneath the waters'
turbulence: roofless walls, foundations, eroded rocks
are crevices of nesting-shelves for creatures
of an underworld where a hollowed-out block
is a brick lid, an eye to blink at a passing cloud

as fish sift through sediment and sailboats roll back
the skin of a lake from moor's edge to moor's edge.

Canada geese sieve through silt, their chinstraps
quiver at each tread of a black foot slipper
on the stone-scattered ground; they chortle, snatch
for scraps left by hikers or bikers. At this inland sea,
the water levels rise or fall with the rain tides, moor
storms

arrive and depart to quench Grains Moss, bogs drain
and seep in rivulets to run the course of the River Don.

The Elders of Laddow Rocks   ii

Sodden boots lace the valley, flecking
each step with a rasp, an echo.

Scything through skeins of mist
old field-systems are discerned
by stone walls, cairns or artful oddities half-lost
in a fall of scree or a sheep-blundered gap.

Pock-marked trees in scant leaf-rags
bow in deference to the speed of the winds.

Drifts of sedge and rush are clamped
in a late-season frost, but the heavy headed
bullrush nods a slow semaphore
flagging the quagmire of peat-brown sores.

All is sepia until a break in the cloud
reveals the grey of ancient gritstone shoulders.

Lamentation

A glut of fruit, too early. A scattering
of petals, the confetti of a fallen

summer. In the long grass, memories
are celandines, thistles scratch, dock leaves

slumber, nettles sting. All the remnants
of those days when we knew buds

would pollinate. And as we played, our carefree
ways made florets on those fragile boughs.

But, in time, our beams collapsed, leaving
eaves bereft of nesting swallows. How cruel

we felt the bite of taunting frost. Unkindly weather:
we say we knew no better, bitter is our loss.

Sonnet to an Urban Fox   iii

At the end of the garden by the hedge,
a ruddy coat shimmers in midday's sun.

The remnants of a vulpine creature, dead,
where flies make mess of wounds, and oh, so young,
I wonder, had you mated, is your spawn
left to forage the bins, to gorge on rats?

Do your young tiptoe the line before dawn
Among the city office squares, apartments,
bleak suburbs designed not for your kind?

Your kin tread bright as they rewild the streets
with mating calls so feared, they are maligned,
accused of darkly deeds. Now your heart's ceased

you dream of sun-warmed walls, this place, your hearth,
your lair, embraced in arms of whiskered earth.

One for Sorrow

Black and white, a long tail, a rudder
for those Chaplinesque moves.

Old photographs, no two-tone clarity,
just misted sepia scenes of gentlefolk.

Plumage, top-hats – it's a proper Sunday.
Gilt-framed, on the mantelpiece. An occasion

to celebrate. All propriety but tints of complexities.
Does singularity constitute simplicity?

He has no accomplice on the lawn.
A special state of grief for a melancholy bird.

At the Foundling Museum

They said
to leave a token,
when I left
my child,
so that, thereafter,
should my circumstance
improve,
I may reclaim
my daughter.

On record,
she'd be a brooch
or ribbon, button,
ticket, coin – the latter
best engraved.
By this way only
she'll be
known as mine.

She is to be renamed.

And if I own
no single thing,
tear a swatch
of clothing, divide,
retain one half
to match the other,
so I may prove
she is the one
I left behind.

They said,
hold tight this fragment of your love.

The final item on the news.

They are preparing for Christmas in New York. A 75-feet Norway Spruce…

My 3-year-old points to the unlit fire. Are you cold? I ask. He runs around the room, flapping his arms.

…has travelled 170 miles south. A crane lifts the tree, and as it tilts, branches splay out, needles spill.

Round eyes are watching.

I open the door of the wood burner. Soot flies in my face.

Experts say it's a Saw-whet owl, an adult male, traumatised by forced migration.

A Little Owl is in the cup of my hands, wings fluttering. How long had it taken to travel from rooftop to stove?

Rockefeller – named on account of the place he was found – has been taken to a sanctuary in the upstate town of Saugerties.

I offer water, try to soothe our *Sooty*, find a box, take him to the vets.

Given a borrowed perch. Rockefeller dreams of hunting in the Oneonta forest.

Sooty has been given fluids. We checked on him throughout the night.

We're very sorry.

In New York, they switch on the lights.

Wreck   iv

Sublingual, she rests on sand
as brine licks the bow
that plied above her ice-block skirts,
now anchor-chained.

Her engines flooded as she flailed
in the freeze of infamy.

Her collared flange, unribbed, propellers
left to languish in their tongues.

Her name still on our lips,
as anaerobic spit
eats through her first-class rooms
– a bathtub of rusticled decay.

Seeking Asylum

You find yourself in a forest where sheep-clothed wolves slip
       sinuously over dead bark, some exult the clouds,
baying to a false moon
       or leaning in to glean the echoes.

On an owl's hoot they bow to the ground in deference,
break their promises, while
       the shallow-rooted yell into a fickle wind.

You listen to hear the words YOU ARE LOVED, but no,
       all whispers hush at the crack of whips, acorns
drop from hoods. And this, the promised land, is where

at dusk, robins shriek in dissonance, squirrels flow in
quick crawl shadow, some are despatched, others
       beguiled by petrichor.

Motion, Emotion

A woman comes out of the kitchen.
She takes a photo of the swing.
'It's for my daughter,' she explains.
'She would love it here!'

Her daughter is nine years old; she is far away,
living in another country with her grandmother.

I look at the swing through the mother's eyes. I see
the girl, how her long legs kick out as she climbs
higher and higher, she pulls back, then forward

again, until her feet touch the under-branches of the tree.
Her clothes flutter, goosebumps rise on her arms,
wind rushes through her open sandals.

'Blackbird singing in the dead of night' v

after Lennon/McCartney.

In the undergrowth, the sub-songs hang
their sadness for the hurt of broken wings.

On blackest nights, we hear the rouse
of medieval hours within a pie baked blind.

Behind the scaffold of a pastry trap, they wait,
as diners clap to see those four and twenty beaks
break through the crust – their flight wings
open-flung to find a dish of dainty fruit.

Again, I listen to the intro, how four chords
dwell in undergrowth, how sub-songs hang
their sadness for the hurt of broken wings.

The Cruelty

A pastime, they say. A noble thing
when the hawk is in the tower
or on the fist.
It hones the skill of the kill.

A legend, they say. A fireside tale
set in a rural landscape where
whip-ready riders urge their dogs
to fleece a fox of its tail.

An antiquarian's delight. A pair of spurs,
a hunter's horn, antlers of a stag,
the souvenirs
of valour in the field.

A tradition, they say, when,
from cage to grave
farmed fledglings
are flung into the sky.

A sport, they say. Always a winner,
a hero, and the victim
with a twisted wing, a hole in the place
of a heart.

Wintering

Shadow lines are scored in parallel folds, creasing the hills, gathering and sinking into a well, a valley, trailing along a risen land, a slight plateau demarcated by lit-up heights. The way markers are posts, alternating from stile to gate, their arrows hinting at a course to be taken, a certainty, a tried and tested route. In places, we follow a watercourse with risen sides that form the pathways, mapped out by the pressing boots, footprints of studs, arrowheads, diamond shapes. There are stone walls, protrusions that act as stiles, and planks laid as bridges over the plenitude of reedy waterholes, bogs chilled in the shadows, iced over. As we travel from curated fields to wilderness—the lines that are of our division—we pass a sign, hanging on a rusted barb, shrouded in the nearside dusk. The letters have fallen, meanings oblique. Are they warnings, or are they the curses of the discontented? A bird passes over a clump of rocks, unseen; we do not recognize its type, not by its shadow or the vibrations it leaves in its wake—the non-sound of a flightless wing. We fear the bleak, the all-seeing hollow, an open mine-shaft, a mist of grey deepened by the half-heard wing beat. Below us, roots are concealed in the peaty ground; they will lie dormant until spring when the warming crust begins to split, triggering our memories, new life, spitting life-force through the watery grounds, new shoots flanking the still frosty paths, a brittle optimism in pale first-growths, an unknown promise, a flag of hope. But for now, the icy air laps the earth with sticky tongues that flicker over the land, and still nothing might emerge.

The Ravens' Tale

from droplets of rain
a pool of light
a mirror
on the woodland floor

reflections
of leaf-fringed sky
no ripple, no wrinkle
at the edge of the silt mouth.

Light filters
through scant gaps
in the dark heart
of the forest,

falters with grace
at the sight of a perfect
silhouette
a raven

spreading its fingered
wings
carrying fables
to our doubting ears.

Yuletide

You are the shadow
of a dusk moon, a trace
of night, of day, as we
tiptoe through twilight stars.

You are a soul, leaning
on a solar tide, riding
rafts of hearth-lit pyres,
waiting for the ebb to glow.

You are the ale
we drink, wassailing
a snow-laced trail where
all roads lead to dust.

Distance

is all

dog wonders
dreaming
through cloud

you call his name

but time alone

is time spent
in another country

Thrift

In Gaelic, 'tonna chladaich' – beach wave; in Welsh,
'clustog fair' Mary's pillow.

Photographing swans

at first light
a ring
reaches
the lakeside
another   is
a heart's knock
a slip   of   white
meets a lingering
shh   on pursed lips
dawn   is the colour
of water   rising mist
lighting   the raw
willowing
of twigs   among reeds
a *mâché*-nest   where
cygnets rest
seamless

The Winding Path

1.
Sphagnum
At the source. Spores.
Trickle, bog moss,
Saturate.
Seep. Leap. A rivulet
into a brooklet grows. Streams flow.

2.
Cotton grass
Dream downhill.
Slow. A worm's wriggle.
Burble.
A headlong flow.
On ground. Reflect. Twinkle.

3.
Heather
Darkling growth, bedrock
slither, cluster, fork.
Applause.
Goldfinches in trees.
Waterfalls.

4.
Reedbed
Cupped into pond.
Lowing. Cow pat.
Cockcrow.
Meander an oxbow.
Irrigate, sluice, escape.

5.
Marram
Muster, swell, final
fluster. Twirl.
Whirlpool.
Sway a hundred tides, lurch
to the moon.

Thrift

She is running, skipping towards the granite headland
where a mighty fall of rock
is the only boundary between land and ocean
– a child running far ahead, her hair

as gold as a cornfield, anorak the blue of sea.
She is at the edge of the cliff
with the dwellers of the sea-slopes
– bird's-foot-trefoil, sea campion, squill.

Wavering heads catch her eye. They look so fragile
– but they are the tough ones, resisting
the Atlantic winds that gather the salt-spray,
sweep along the cliffs, scouring

all in their wake, leaving only the hardiest
– stonecrop, sea-spurrey, vetch.
The path is narrow, she is an only child
of nine years of age, alone, and yet

wanting to be more alone, for the world
to be her and cliff and sky, to be surrounded
by sea pinks, buffeted
by the elements, cradled in thrift.

Empath

Through the kitchen window,
            clouds unpierced
                        by haw or thorn.

A sparrow hawk,
          eyes lichen bold
                    in the dull light.

Her cells suspended
          on a telegraph wire,
                    mine in my stilled hand.

Grass riffles/reveals/hides
          breasts quicken
                    eyes stretched in the rain.

As fields unmap,
          feathers fletch
                    as her tail tilts.

In my hand
          the spoon is a helicopter
                    heading for my child's mouth.

Air squeezed
          between her wings,
                    she dives onto her prey.

Wasp

Wearing your bee-like cloak, a builder's mask,
you work all through summer, your task,

to build for your Queen a spittle-spit nest.
In your final days you're August's pest –

around my face – neck, lips, ears – you are pissed
on life's decay, slow-fused, your wings half-list

in a blundering search while you feed free
on the over-ripe fruits fallen from the apple tree.

Reservoir Fish vi

I am the first fish to arrive. A buzzard in the sky
is watching over the men in the town of tin.

At night, the labourers are in their iron huts, drinking
beer in shacks, as valley folk seep into the shadows,

ghost children play, dogs bark at flies, farmworkers
go about their day among the five-tonne blocks.

On Sundays they pray in church for the land they will
not leave without a promise to preserve the tower.

The packhorse bridge already under the mason's hammer.
Boulders sealed in cement form Gothic dams

only bombs can breach. Water levels rise. I swim around
the steeple where things are bright and beautiful.

Borderlands

Brittle stars scatter, falling
into deep pools.
Seals finfoot the lapping
      drawing their blubber bodies
onto the rocks
         huge pods of bladderwrack
watch a kayaker
     twist the paddles in
and out, heading towards the edge
where the scaly gatekeeper
dwells beneath the reef.
A serpent's tale flicks
        from under a shelf of rock.
A curious breath rises
a storm shudders in the deep
as the horizon draws night
from a thin line of light.
A crested head rises,
eyes at the rim of the world.

Tea with the Bal Maidens   vii

Seabed boulders
roll roll roll
over their heads
metalliferous
seams creak and scream.

'There's plenty of 'sten''
the miners call
to them
on the surface
who lift,
haul, pick, break, sep-
arate the ore
to find
the crack
that binds
the tin.

They dress the ore:
chant, sing, swig,
quenched
with mugwort tea.

On Board

With the heel of his hand, the plane
slices the wood held tight in the vice.
Shaven curls are golden waves.
A sea of sawdust laps at his feet
                        – he bends down to stroke the cat.

On a high shelf is a dry dock
for a perfect ship in a bottle, her hull
encased in glass, sails yellowed,
she bears a rig, spars, raised mast
                        -– a black cat sits proudly at the prow

like the one he rescued from the streets
of a foreign port, permitted on board
to catch the rats and mice.
The fine hairs on his hands are white crests
                        – the cat purrs to his touch.

The distance between us

a motor breaks
      water ripples
            propellers whirr
                  bite into the silence
                        between blades

uncharted course
      swirls released
            putter forwards
                  leaving safe harbours
                        unfurling the waves

1816   viii

'The Year without Summer'.

On Mr Turner's canvas the sun sets
sap green, cadmium yellow, smudge-umber.

Mount Tambor's magma risen, molten ash
and dust block out the sun. Mary Shelley
incubates her Frankenstein as spectres roam
the ruined fields, crops rust. There is no harvest.
The call to revolt is 'Bread or Blood!'

As snow falls in flakes of burnt sienna
the artist's pallet records a climate cursed.

2022

A Year with Summer

It is hard to believe
in extinction
but here we are
communing
in slow grief
watching tulips
in gardens
open their cups
to the burning sun
as we drive by
on a highway
turning down
the drone
to discern
the melody
of songbirds.

In aestivation

Late on in
hibernation
a sense
of movement
from above.
Feet,
tyres,
a scratch
of claw?
We know
only
light from
dark, how
soil sticks
like clay,
like family
who
roam
the
loam,
to
plough
a new
field.

Travelling with Old Man's Beard

(aka Clematis Vitalbae)

When the cold winds of autumn blow, we shake
permed heads, rattle seedheads, disseminate

across hedgerows. Like travellers we roam,
wily, our freedom sought in light or gloam.

Way back, in the Stone Age we tagged along,
or grew by stealth. We are true vagabonds.

Our sinews hold the sheaves of corn, baskets
made of woven stems carry a harvest

to your homes. We survived; we have no fear.
So long we've lived, we have stars in our beard.

A Shift of Light

The roe deer saw me, and I saw her.
We froze.
Her side eye encompassed the whole of me.

A silent second, a dialogue
of tension, a tête-à-tête. I was in awe.
But for her – was I friend or foe?

Her beauty in the shift of light, the red
brown of her still-summer coat
graced the dappled shades of autumn.

As I held out my hand she leapt into the forest,
leaving no tracks to prove my witness,

To the Spirit of the Wood, Green Man, Green Woman ix

Let the bark fall from your wrinkled cheek, open your
sleepy eyes, lift your feet from littered floors when you
feel the drub of a chainsaw's trill. They have come to let
your green blood flow. You have no defence against their
beat; their reasoning is for growth, not the leafy kind, but
for profit.

While you are still able, collect a small branch from every
tree, a sapling growth, an acorn, beechnut, chestnut, the
sycamore's seed. Call all creatures from the dappled
wood, keep them safely in the deep of your pockets. Hold
tight your cloak as the stripping lights pierce your sides,
the scent of wood-burn smothers your subtle scent of
petrichor. Soon your load will be heavier with a pack of
carbon on your back. For sustenance, you have the dust of
the bared earth while your deep cuts weep for oak, elm,
ash, birch, linden, and larch. Your tears are their sap. Now
you'll walk in open fields left fallow, cross scarred rock,
cropped moor, your roots severed on the blade-turned
earth. You'll slip on the ice of winter, the pools that never
drain will rot you to the core.

I beg you, please do not forget the forest, those years of
living, breathing, stretching to a canopy of sky. Remember
your resilience. Before the final nails, breathe deep, speak
the old spells, tell tales of magic, return the fiery eye to the
heart of the forest. Hold out your arms to starving birds,
whistle to the crows who cry on broken boughs, open
your pores for insects, feel the fungi's tickle in the soil,
sing the songs of the wood, help us regenerate.

Biometrics

only a tender
       gaze knows
              the meaning
                     of the rings
                            the marks of
                                   seasons

                                            hardships

                               recorded
                        in a cylinder
                of bark
           circles
       distilled
in grain
       scars of years
           and all the
                unfinished
                     secrets
                            held in sap.

By the River Dwyfor

Under the great umbrella of a beech, the river shillies
around rocks as they resist the current.

Some are boulders; sturdy, unyielding, others
are dry, moss-covered, but all as dull as the slip-grey sky.

Around me the air sings, the wind carries a song of a
lullaby.

I rest at the feet of the great trunk – all its years of growth,
pock-marked by seasons, challenged by lichen.

Leaves criss-cross each other above me, not quite
touching, allowing air to filter, opening a multitude of
crevices for the sky to enter.

Air. Water. Leaf. Neither surface nor place, unowned by
all.

A rope hangs from a branch, knotted at the end, slung
over a strong limb, ready to be swung across the river in a
child's leap.

Ivy graces the rocks on the bank.

Moss-cladding is deep, green, velvet.

Himalayan Balsam sways its sex, opening to the damp air.

On the far bank, brambles etch their shapes, stretching their feelers.

A moment of sun breaks through the cloud and the colours change, quick-bright water magnifying the stony bed, catching the tails of ghost-minnows darting in and out of the shallows.

Leaves, grass, a rickety fence – all trying out new colours from the artist's pallet.

Downstream the water is feather-white, leaping over rocks; an ash tree waves flags as if, at any moment, it will take-off, each leaf buffeting one against the other, jostling, vying for a glimpse of the sun.

A tiny black and red winged creature searches the length of my trouser leg.

My boots crunch on the sprinkling of beechmast around the tree.

With my back against the trunk, in my nest of numbness, my human bones are flesh deep as they take root in tree and river and rock.

Enraptured

We listen to the flautist in the arched doorway of the church. The boy takes the silver coin, walks towards the busker, drops it into the hat.

whistling winds
leaves shift

The boy runs, weaving in and out of the headstones, the melody follows in his slipstream. His mother calls through the lychgate, but the boy is enchanted.

Casting a line into the river
notes flutter

Sage

'Cultivate poverty like a garden herb, like sage.'
Henry David Thoreau

fish leap
ever growing circles
reach the bank

And still….

by sea-spewn waste
        a reek of salt

bright glow buoys
        watch surfers

ride the outlet
        slack-sheet boats

wait by bleached jetties
        empty creels

piled on neon-waves
        litter rattles

a slipway as we yawn
        the deepest blues

lace-petals
        on a porcelain sky.

Sky Road to Slimbridge x

Eye to eye you rise to the rush, lapping
at thermals, hungry for height.

Aloft, your cruising wings are kept
within an iris, a span of sails.

A snowstorm slaps the Siberian tundra.
It's -25 degrees. Icebergs shift on a feisty sea.

Artic Foxes eye the sleek
of your trail. A wolf snarls.

Your Bewick's crew is drawn
into the slipstream, a point of V.

Skimming the flatlands, stunned by turbines,
wings made mute or sizzled in the wirelines.

Sprayed with a shotgun's shrapnel
–one slap and a flap is a falling to earth.

Gliding over flood lands,
crossing a strip of sea where

thermals lift you over the white-wing cliffs
to the place of a shotless sky.

Truth

is in the wonder
of magnificence
where sky reflects
a sea of light
patterns of blue
dissolve
horizons
a cool palette
casts a tide to
mirror
the moon

Unfastening

Boats rest on the mud
    of the harbour floor
        sea chains uncurl

anchors half-released
    are grip-fixed
        by denoting buoys

a black-backed gull
    circles a plastic float
        nylon ropes fray

the bi-daily flow
    lustres a patina
        on the rocks

as sea-reeds
    stroke a palimpsest
        of prints

I leave my shadow-wings
    the span of
        my open beak

a sedimentary snapshot
    captured in the drift
        of my unmooring

where the lee of a ripple
        is a collar of sand
                swept by the ebb.

haar

caught in a mist

fibres   on a barb

brisk winds   loosening fear

spinning   on a web

in a storm's eye

to rest   unstilled

to sink   below

a neck retracts

in the unrest

a ceaseless   shiver

flicker flight

skin-flitter

seeking   the sleep

of river giver

as paths   evaporate

                    drip
                    run
                    slip

falling

gaps

of shadow

Funeral of the Cailleach xi

There's no sorcery in the clachan, no fallen
tear in the kirk. As we grieve, we offer
a tribute to yore, to the ancient forces that
moulded the mountains, carved the ice-dint valleys.

Did we expel you, oh, spell maker?

Decades passed before we noticed you had fled.
Quick at the turn, leaving only the whirls
of your heels, footprints of blood in the mud.

Is it too late to stamp your staff on the ground
to banish the early Spring, to herd the deer
back to the forests, to howl with the wolfpack?

Rise, rise, let your breath paint the leaves
with a mist of ice, flee from the dawn of a rising
sun, speak with the arrows of dark. Do not
let Winter retire before the equinox pyre.

Elder

My weight is that of an average sheep, an orangutan,
a mountain lion, a spotted hyaena, a Timor deer,
with a full set of osseous tissue, marrow, mineral,

sinew, blood. My ribs, fixed to the strut of my spine,
create a fragile cage around my heart. As I swing through
the trees, my doe eye shifts from side to side, scanning
the forest floor,

but I'm not on the look-out for a mate, nor do I wish to
flash my rippled/wrinkled canine pelt. My fertility is
shed, my cat-beast still protects my brood, scattered in a
far-off place;

there'll be no more hatchlings from my nest. My blood
thins as it flows, it slows, spots of ageing ink. My skin
is the paper on which I write the density of my bones.

Wolf Woman

The verges are redolent with the aromas
of creatures: traces of urine, fur, scat.

Her bones bear down to the earth
as if she too will bleed into the soil.

She feels a flicker of the hunt, a chase,
but her eyes meet only bare ground.

She stifles a yowl as pressure gathers,
she feels a tremor, a clench, a cramp.

By day she follows the trail of shrew and mouse,
but at night she raises her cup to the moon

– her wolf genes insist. Even in the civilised world,
there is wilderness held at the end of a leash.

At last, a slippery relief. But sometimes,
there is grief in that iron scent.

The Display

The tools are on the kitchen table:
scissors, shallow vase, secateurs.

Gathered in a trug:
two red peonies, lavender, rosemary, white rose.

She begins the arrangement:
cuts, trims, pushes each stem into the oasis.

Her apron strings are tied
– a bow around her emptiness.

Frost Feathers

The velvet petals of plucked
anemones are purple in this winter
of grief, crocuses bloom
in plumes of light, a flight foretelling
of a long winter when storm-split trees etch
the riverbank as they sail towards
an estuary of ghosts.

Hope

a half-sunk plant pot
    plastic wrapping
        last year's bracken
            an ornamental fairy
                pond clutter

flag iris push upwards
    green blades dare
        sharpening the light
            soon yellow flowers
                will tilt towards the sun

I lift the water
    silver drips from my hand
        the colour of peat
            below the surface
                frogspawn

Nurture

step

into a puddle of sky

lean   into the ripples

touch   the bark   of an oak

describe   the carved heart

follow   the sign   of an arrow

gather the veined   leaf

of horse-chestnut in the palm of your hand

plant   your soles   in the silence

look up   to the canopy

a webbed umbrella

absorbs   the ether

while Earth holds you

safe   you will not fall

where roots embrace

seeds ignite

Canopy

You lie on the forest floor, gazing with pain
up into the branches of Monterey Pines, seeing how
ravens skim the tops, then disappear. You close your eyes,
drawn upwards as if a magnet plucks your body, head,
breast, stomach, knees, and feet. You are separated
from the part of you that holds your pain. The ground
beneath is a mattress of moss, a safe place
to leave the underside of your body.

High up in the branches, you are held by fine
leaves and twigs. The sky, a spectrum – all shades
of silver, blue, and creamy whites, where clouds form
familiar shapes, then shift and drift away. You look
down from your nesting place, to see the scoop made
by the weight of your body, the place you left all
pain behind. There, is the outline of your spine.
See how each vertebra is filled with tiny flowers.

without the skill of flight
dream-healing

Somewhere

Without the signpost
she would never have known the route.
The wall is stretched with webs, each corner pegged on a
crack or tethered on a slight branch. A dropped stitch here
and the circle bulges, agility questioned.
To avoid a break, she pushes aside the Traveller's Joy,
climbs over the stile, smiles, and calls to the dog as she
lifts the wooden post to let him through.
Woman and dog stare at the view from this top field.
She breathes deep.
Across the valley
the bracken fields are the colour of acorn.
Rows of newly planted birch are cloistered in tubes of
plastic defying those who'd steal their bark or reach up for
fresh-formed leaves beyond their sleeves.

Down the steep hill, side-stepping potholes, minding the
edges, holding her bones in place, slipping in the mud,
balancing on stones that tip with her shifting weight.
Distraction.
The dog's ears lift as the grouse chortle
screeching away in the heather.
A single feather floats in the air.
She carries on down and down and down to the river.

She can't wait to take off her socks and boots, to feel the
ice-cool silk around her feet.
She knows this place by the scent of rotting beech, the
way water sounds as it runs over moss-capped stones.
Even the split wooden bridge exudes a scent.
It is so deep, so shady here in this valley.
She thinks about the spider crocheting her way from
stone to stone, spinning a fragile kaleidoscope
to entrance the sun.

Moths

The moon on the sill
of our bare embrace
so tender
as we trace
our hearts
of powdered wings

the flight of the
night on a frosted
pane, the tryst
of breath where beads
are jewels of love
in the morning light

where you and
I, a brace of wings
our love cleaved
as one, no slipknot
now, fully melded,
we have grown as one.

After it's all over

I'll be whatever I wish to be.

I'll choose a wren's body, wear the feathers
       of a goldcrest, a jay's blue plume behind each ear.

I'll fly with lapwings in the sky, leave poems
       in waves where contrails used to be.

I'll walk the hills in a deer's skin, file my nails
       on the tough oak bark, buff them on a mossy crop.

My feet will be woven leaves, my soles the colours
       of lichen as I spring across the summer fields.

Then, when I'm tired, I'll rest on the riverbanks
       with the rats and mice and voles.

I'll sleep in their earth-rich skin.
       But when winter comes

I'll sparkle in a gown of ice,
       dance across the spangled earth.

I'll be whatever I wish to be.

End Notes

i The Monarch of Mabon. The Monarch butterflies travel great distances and are a rare immigrant to Britain, but occasionally seen in the south-west.

ii The Elders of Laddow Rocks. These dramatic cliffs can be seen following the Pennine Way from Crowden OS grid ref SK072992

iii Sonnet of an Urban Fox. According to the London Wildlife Trust there are 10,000 foxes in London. Some see urban foxes as a kind of revenge on city-dwellers for voting to ban foxhunting

iv Wreck. A poem inspired by the wreck of the RMS Titanic. Shipwrecks are a source of marine pollution, damaging ocean habitat with contents, cargo, and fuel.

v 'Blackbird singing in the dead of night'. A favourite song by The Beatles that brings grief along with its melody.

vi Reservoir Fish. The controversial flooding of the villages of Derwent and Ashopton were carried out to provide reservoirs of water to the cities. To house the workers, a village of corrugated iron homes was constructed, known as Tin Town, and since dismantled.

vii Tea with the Bal Maidens. Employed in large numbers from about 1770 until 1860 women and children worked in hazardous conditions in the mines of Devon and Cornwall

viii 1816. A volcanic event thought to be caused by the 1815 eruption of Mount Tambora, led to winter temperatures during the following summers and severe crop failure across Europe and the Northern Hemisphere.

ix To the Spirit of the Wood. Large swathes of ancient woodland and irreplaceable habitat were lost during Phase 1 of the HS2 project.

x Sky Road to Slimbridge. Bewick's swans migrate from northern Russia to the UK every year facing many dangers. Their recent delayed arrival is thought to be due to climate change.

xi In Gaelic, the Cailleach is a divine hag and ancestor, associated with the creation of the landscape and with the weather, and especially storms and winter.

Alison Lock - Biography

Alison Lock was born in Devon and, after three decades living in West Yorkshire, is now based in North Wales. She has published fiction, non-fiction and poetry in many literary reviews and magazines, and is the author of several collections and pamphlets, the most recent being *Unfurling*, Palewell Press 2022. A poetic sequence of personal transformation was broadcast on the BBC Radio 3 programme *Between the Ears: Lure*. For more information go to: www.alisonlock.com

Palewell Press

Palewell Press is an independent publisher handling poetry, fiction and non-fiction with a focus on books that foster Justice, Equality and Sustainability.
The Editor can be reached on
enquiries@palewellpress.co.uk
